ANIMAL MATTERS

LIFE FILES

ANIMAL MATTERS

PHILIP STEELE

Evans

EVANS BROTHERS LTD

Evans Brothers Limited
2A Portman Mansions
Chiltern Street
London W1M 1LE

Produced by Foundry Design and Production, a part of
The Foundry Creative Media Company Ltd
Crabtree Hall, Crabtree Lane
Fulham, London, SW6 6TY

British Library Cataloguing in Publication Data
Steele, Philip
    Animal Matters – (Life Files)
    I. Animals – Juvenile literature
    I. Title
    590

ISBN 0 237 52081 8

Thanks to Douglas Wells for help with picture research and Camilla de la Bédoyère
for consultancy work on this book.

For permission to reproduce copyright material, the author and publishers gratefully
acknowledge the following:

Impact Photo: Robin Laurance 13
RSPCA Photo Library: 16, 19, 51, E.A. Janes 36, 40, Andrew Linscott 17, Tim Martin 24, Duncan I. McEwan 52, Phillip
Meech 18, Jonathan Plant 23, Martin Potter 35, Alex Warman 14
Still Pictures: Dianne Blell 28, Joerg Boethling 11, Nigel Dickinson 30, Mark Edwards 12, 44, EIA 29, Dylan Garcia 55, 56,
Michel Gunther 9, 21, Malcolm S. Kirk 47, Klein/Hubert 37, Detlef Konnerth 7, Tristan Lafranchis 15, Bruno Marielle 33,
Muriel Nicolotti 54, Thomas Raupach 10, Stewart Weir 57
Topham: 48

CONTENTS

1. Animal attitudes   7

2. All God's creatures?   11

3. Cruelty and captivity   15

4. Environment and wildlife   23

5. Hunting, fishing and whaling   29

6. On the farm   35

7. Meat or murder?   41

8. In the laboratory   45

9. Animal rights?   51

10. Animals and activists   55

Organisations and Helplines   59

Websites   60

Index   61

ANIMAL ATTITUDES

Animal matters make news. Hunting, fishing, factory farming, eating meat, laboratory experiments, animal welfare, wildlife conservation are all headline issues. How should we treat the animals which share the planet with us? Every one of us has to decide sooner or later, for our attitudes towards animals will affect our diet, the clothes we wear and the products we buy.

> **Man is the only animal that blushes, or needs to.**
>
> Mark Twain (1835–1910), US writer

> **The key concept in regulating our treatment of other species is that of welfare, not of rights. If we treat animals as if they had rights, we mistreat them. We impose upon them a standard of conduct that they can neither emulate nor understand.**
>
> Countryside Movement, Charter on the Welfare of Animals, UK Countryside Alliance

It is difficult to resolve animal issues. Human attitudes towards animals are deeply complex. Different values may set apart families, sections of society, cultures and nations. However, even the views held by one individual may seem contradictory. A farmer may lavish care and attention on a lamb, and then enjoy eating it as chops. A hunter may love the hound which kills the fox, even though both animals are members of the dog family.

Calves and other livestock are often transported for many miles in cramped conditions before being slaughtered. This practice is just one of the many animal matters under debate.

ANIMALS AND US

What do we have in common with animals? What sets us apart? Scientists classify human beings as mammals: warm-blooded creatures which give birth to live young and feed them with mothers' milk. We are in the sub-group called primates, which includes apes and monkeys. In fact, our closest relatives in the animal kingdom are chimpanzees.

As well as posing difficult moral questions which we have to deal with as individuals, animal matters affect society as a whole. They must be considered whenever we discuss the way in which we use the planet's resources, methods of feeding the world's growing population and the economies of most countries in the world.

Whatever we *feel* about animals, we have to acknowledge that we are dependent upon them. The Earth's ecology is a complex network of relationships. The lives of plants, animals and humans are all interdependent; their future and ours are closely tied together.

> " Those who wish to pet and baby wild animals 'love' them. But those who respect their natures and wish to let them live normal lives, love them more. "
>
> Edwin Way Teale (1899–1980), American writer and naturalist

Question
What confusions or contradictions do the following statements highlight?

"The Worldwide Fund for Nature chose a cuddly panda as its logo – but they didn't choose a toad or a slug, did they?"
Mark, animal rights activist (18)

"Look good in leather."
Advertisement

"Man's best friend is health threat."
Newspaper report on dog mess in children's playground

Humans and animals share the same origins. Fossil remains discovered around the world show that over millions of years, animals evolved or developed into different forms, each best suited to the conditions in which they found themselves. Today, humans remain greatly outnumbered by other life forms, such as insects. However, humans are successful in another way. They are the most intelligent creatures ever to have existed on Earth. They have the ability to change the environment in which they live in ways that animals cannot.

> " There is no fundamental difference between man and the higher animals in their mental faculties…. The difference in mind between man and the higher animals, great as it is, is certainly one of degree and not of kind. "
>
> Charles Darwin (1809–82), English scientist

Charles Darwin's book, *On the Origin of the Species*, explained his theory of evolution: that humans had developed over thousands of years from ape-like creatures. We share certain characteristics with this chimpanzee.

Our modern attitudes towards animals have their roots in ancient times. About 40,000 years ago, humans hunted other animals for food and for their skins, which they used to make shelter and clothing. Unlike simply gathering food or scavenging, hunting required the strength of groups of people. Hunting requires cooperation and communication and so it may have helped humans develop strong social groups.

Over time, humans began to tame and breed animals, such as dogs, horses and cattle. They discovered that it was possible to improve the quality and health of the animals by only allowing the best ones, with the most favourable characteristics – such as woolly fleeces – to breed. This is called selective breeding, and it heralded a new era in human and animal relationships.

For modern scientists, the next logical step in selective breeding is to make choices and fundamental changes at the genetic level. This is called genetic engineering. Will it really improve the world we live in, or is there a danger in scientists 'playing God'? How much do we care about, or understand, the implications of what is being done to other animal species?

> ❝ **Farmers ... are the founders of human civilisation.** ❞
>
> Daniel Webster (1782–1852), US lawyer and politician

Farmers have been using selective breeding to improve the quality and health of their livestock for many years. Now scientists have taken the first steps towards genetic engineering. What effect will this have on the world in which we live?

Chapter 2

ALL GOD'S CREATURES?

Many philosophies and religions are concerned with the way people treat animals. Can they offer us any guidelines or an acceptable code of conduct?

Today, approximately three million Indians follow the Jain religion. A Jain holy man has few possessions, but the ones he does own are devoted to preserving all forms of life:

- A Jain is a vegetarian.
- He has a cloth to strain any microscopic creatures from the water he drinks.
- He has a mask over his mouth to prevent the accidental swallowing of a fly.
- He has a brush or fly-whisk to sweep away any beetles from the path on which he walks.
- He may not farm, in case the plough kills a worm.

Many people would find it difficult to accept all these conditions as a practical model for their daily lives, but the Jain philosophy does at least demonstrate a consistency in attitude towards animals. The logic has been applied to practical political tactics, notably in the beliefs of the great Indian leader, Mahatma Gandhi, who adopted a policy of non-violence in his struggle to free India from British rule. Gandhi believed that respect for all life should be a characteristic of humanity worldwide.

> 66 **The greatness of a nation and its moral progress can be judged by the way its animals are treated.** 99
>
> Mahatma Gandhi (1869–1943), Indian campaigner

A Jain at worship. The Jain faith expresses stringent guidelines on how animals should be treated.

SACRED ANIMALS

A deep respect for all forms of life is also often felt by hunters,even though they kill animals for food. Perhaps this is because they depend on the animals for their way of life. Prehistoric hunters used to dress in skins and horns and pray to the animals' spirits before the hunt. Australian Aboriginals and many African peoples adopted animals as the magical emblem – or 'totem' – of their clan or tribe.

Even after they had learned to farm, the ancient Egyptians continued to believe that many wild animals were sacred, and their gods were pictured with the heads of animals and birds. Some religions today still sacrifice animals, a practice which is intended to honour the spirit of life rather than destroy it.

RELIGIOUS TEACHINGS, MORAL CODES

Most religions which teach that God created the world also claim that God made both humans and animals. Some religions hold the belief that God gave souls to animals as well as humans. However, few religions give the two equal status.

African children performing dances dressed as forest animals. Such ceremonies are still common in many parts of the world.

Jewish and Christian scriptures make it clear that although animals were made by God, humans were given dominance over them. Even so, many religious thinkers have emphasised human respect for animal life rather than control over it.

> **And God said, Let us make Man in our own image, after our likeness: and let them have dominion over the fish of the sea, and over the fowl of the air, and over the cattle, and over all the earth, and over everything that creepeth upon the earth.**
>
> The Bible: Genesis I: verses 25–26

Non-religious people may care just as passionately as religious people about the way in which humans treat animals. They may base their views on ethics, on practical science, or on personal feelings and emotions.

REBORN - AS ANIMALS?

One idea that has been around for thousands of years is that when humans die, their spirit can be reborn in another body. The Greek philosopher Pythagorus (*c.* 580–500 BC) believed in this 'transmigration of souls'. Hindus, Buddhists and Jains all believe that humans can be reborn as animals. This idea obviously affects the way in which they view animals. Whether you accept transmigration or not, it could be argued that there is some common ground here with the scientific view that all living creatures share a common origin and are therefore related.

> **The soul is the same in all living creatures, although the body of each is different.**
>
> Hippocrates (*c.* 460–377 BC), Greek physician

ANIMAL TABOOS

In many religions, there are taboos about the way animals are treated, slaughtered or eaten. For example, Jews and Muslims may not eat pork. At one time, Christians were banned from eating any meat at all during the festival of Lent – but they could eat fish. Many such taboos have their roots in prehistoric times and are related either to tribal animal totems or to ancient practices of health and hygiene. Traditions like these give a social group a sense of cultural identity and offer individuals a sense of belonging.

Many religions have laws about the treatment of animals, how they are slaughtered for food, and which meats they can eat; Jews, for example, are forbidden from eating pork.

21ST CENTURY WORRIES

The ways in which animals live have changed greatly in the last 50 years. The animal matters that concern us today are not always dealt with by existing moral guidelines. Many of the emotions we feel about animals date back to the days when humans hunted for their food, and most religions and philosophies date from an age when the majority of people still lived in the countryside.

Today many people have never seen a wild animal and know very little about the ways in which animals are raised on farms. The only animals they know are pets. In an inner city, a young child might never make the connection between a milk shake and a cow, between a sausage and the slaughter of a pig.

In the early twenty-first century there is no clear, general agreement as to how humans should treat animals. Religious or moral guidelines may be a help to many, but they vary greatly and are rarely consistent in themselves. In the end, it is up to you as an individual to look at the whole range of animal matters and decide where you will draw the line.

> **"Perhaps the time has come to formulate a moral code which would govern our relations with the great creatures of the sea as well as those on dry land. "**
>
> Jacques Yves Cousteau (1910–97),
> French underwater explorer

Find out!
The Qur'an is the holy book of Islam. Find out what it says about animals and the ways in which they should be treated by humans. Which animals may be eaten by Muslims?

In India, cows are treated as sacred by Hindus. Religious beliefs about animals vary greatly around the world. They may provide a starting point for thinking about the way we treat animals.

CRUELTY AND CAPTIVITY

Humans use animals for all sorts of purposes – on the farm, for example, or in the laboratory. Sometimes the animals suffer as a result of such activities, and many people say that this is cruel, whatever the reason. However, some cruelty towards animals seems to have no other motive than pleasure. Some people seem to enjoy inflicting pain upon animals; they may tie fireworks to a cat's tail or torment a dog. In ancient Rome, excited crowds would spend a holiday afternoon watching wild animals fighting in a stadium, just as we might go to the cinema.

In some countries today, chained bears are prodded and hit so that they will 'dance' before an audience on the street. Cock fighting is still popular even in countries where it is illegal.

Question
Why are some people cruel to animals? Are they acting out of a basic human instinct?

> **Until he extends his circle of compassion to include all living things, man will not himself find peace.**
> Albert Schweitzer (1875–1965), German doctor, philosopher and theologian

An Asian bear is made to 'dance' before a crowd in the street. This type of performance was once common, but has now been banned in many countries as cruel and demeaning.

SPORT OR CRUELTY?

Bullfighting is a popular form of entertainment in Spain, Portugal, south-western France and Latin America. During a session, or *corrida*, a bull is released into the ring. It is first speared by horseriders called *picadores*, then pierced by darts, and finally faced by a *matador* before being killed with a sword. *Matadores* risk their lives and many are badly gored by enraged bulls. About 30 million Spaniards go to watch a bullfight each year, and tens of thousands of bulls, specially bred for the ring, are killed in this way.

- Some supporters of bullfighting see it as an ancient ritual, rather like a religious sacrifice or a hunting ceremony, or like seeing a tragic play in the theatre. It is believed to honour the bull as well as human bravery. Most followers see it as an art rather than as a sport.

- Opponents of bullfighting say the custom may well be ancient, but that it indulges our most savage instincts. Bullfighting demeans the bull and causes it immense distress. This is neither art nor sport, they say, but a barbaric and cruel spectacle which should be outlawed.

Question

Bullfighting provides pleasure for millions of people and employment for thousands. The cattle end up being killed anyway. Does this balance the arguments for and against the sport?

Bullfighting is an ancient – and still very popular – form of entertainment; bulls are bred especially for this purpose.

ANIMAL WELFARE

Before 1822 there were no laws to protect animals against cruelty. Then Britain passed one of the world's first animal welfare laws, banning cruelty to livestock. The first animal welfare organisation was formed in 1824. It later became known as the Royal Society for the Prevention of Cruelty to Animals (RSPCA). Ironically, human slavery was not abolished in the British Empire until 1833.

Nowadays our society does not consider cruelty to animals to be acceptable – or does it? Cruelty may be less visible on the streets and it is often limited or prohibited by law. However, animal welfare officers still come across cases of individual cruelty. Some of these are intentional, others are caused by an individual's ignorance, thoughtlessness or neglect. An officer's job might include:

- Capturing a stray cat or dog.
- Curing or putting down sick animals.
- Finding homes for unwanted pets.
- Rescuing water birds which have swallowed fishing line and weights.
- Checking if gamekeepers are illegally trapping or poisoning birds of prey.
- Investigating reports of neglected or starving farm animals.

An RSPCA welfare officer checking standards at a livestock market.

- The RSPCA receives about 100,000 reports of cruelty each year in England and Wales.
- 1.3 million people call the RSPCA for advice each year.

Question
Should animal welfare organisations put down unwanted pets, if no home can be found for them?

Find out!
What laws were there covering cruelty to animals when the RSPCA was first founded in 1824, and how have the laws changed since then?

Most people admire the hard and valuable work carried out by individual animal welfare officers. But many of the larger welfare organisations come under criticism from the public.

- Some critics think that the established animal welfare organisations should be much more radical. They want to see them confront industries and farms which, they say, are abusing animals on a larger scale than ever before. Organisations such as the RSPCA point out that they do now campaign on a wide range of controversial issues, from hunting to farming methods.

- Other critics complain that animal welfare organisations already interfere too much. For example, Britain's RSPCA condemns the 'docking' or surgical removal of pet dogs' tails as an unnecessary and cruel mutilation. Some dog breeders say that docking is not cruel. They believe that docking prevents long tails getting damaged later in life and that it is more hygienic for long-haired breeds. They suggest that the RSPCA is squandering the funds it raises as a charity by opposing this practice.

> 66 **Surgical operations for the purpose of modifying the appearance of an animal or for other non-curative purposes shall be prohibited ... in particular ... the docking of tails ... de-clawing and de-fanging.** 99
>
> European Convention for the Protection of Pet Animals (1987)

An RSPCA officer checking the condition of a dog. The RSPCA takes a strong stand against the docking of dogs' tails.

ANIMALS IN TRANSIT

Farm animals are often moved thousands of kilometres from where they were raised to other countries, where they are then slaughtered for food. They are transported live so that the meat will be fresh, but they may suffer extreme hardship on the journey. The European Convention on animal transportation demands that:

• Animals are inspected by an official veterinary inspector before leaving.
• Vehicles provide space, ventilation and protection from the weather.
• Vehicles are clean and provided with litter.
• Animals are fed and watered at least once every 24 hours.
• There are no unecessary delays. Animal loads should be given priority at borders, marshalling yards etc.

Airport staff are familiar with animals freighted by air arriving in overcrowded crates and inadequate conditions, distressed or even dead. Where might the blame lie?
• The law?
• The airline companies?
• Airport inspectors?
• Traders in pets and zoo animals?
• A lack of education in the countries of origin?
• The general public?

NEGLECT AND IGNORANCE

Animals need active care whether on the farm, in the home, or in captivity. They need feeding, watering, grooming and mucking out. If animals are neglected they can starve, become ill, spread disease to other animals and to humans, too. Neglect, often the result of thoughtlessness or ignorance, can be every bit as cruel as beating or torturing an animal.

Question
When does a puppy make a good Christmas present – and when not?

Neglect is often as cruel to animals as physical mistreatment. All tame animals need properly looking after.

EXOTIC PETS

A recent growth in the popularity of exotic pets, such as spiders, lizards and snakes, has caused problems for pet-shop owners. They may not have the expert knowledge required to care for these unusual creatures, nor may their customers. The British RSPCA had 68 traders convicted of abuse of exotic pets between 1998 and 1999.

Question
Why do people want to own exotic pets?

ZOOS AND CIRCUSES

Wild animals have long been fashion items. In the Middle Ages, kings would show off by sending each other gifts of unusual wild animals such as giraffes or elephants. They started collections, or menageries, of animals. The public would come and gaze in wonder at the outlandish beasts. As the world opened up, elephants and tigers became much more familiar to people. Often, though, they were beaten and forced to learn circus tricks. Nevertheless, circuses and zoos enabled ordinary people to witness animals they would never have

seen otherwise and promoted a growing interest in the natural world.

Today, the better zoos try to recreate the animals' natural living conditions. We know much more about animals' needs and can keep them relatively healthy and happy. They are given more space to exercise. They receive a more balanced, natural diet and better veterinary care. They may be given space to hide from the public gaze. Animals, like humans, need mental as well as physical activity, so apes may be encouraged to play and learn.

But why keep animals in zoos at all? Their behaviour in captivity is often so different from that in the wild, that observation of animal behaviour in zoos is of limited scientific application. And in ethical terms could it not be considered just another form of imprisonment?

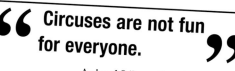

" Circuses are not fun for everyone. "

Animal Liberation Organisation of Australia

However, a good case can be made out for some of the jobs being undertaken by zoos today. Firstly, many of them become breeding centres for endangered animals, which are then released back into the wild. This has to be a long-term operation and must be combined with measures taken in the wild: there is little point releasing animals in this way, if they remain under threat in their natural habitats.

OPERATION ORYX

The Arabian oryx, a long-horned antelope which lives on the desert fringes of the Arabian peninsula, was hunted to the verge of extinction in the 1950s and 60s.

1962 Three wild oryx were flown to the USA. A breeding programme was started at zoos in Phoenix, Arizona and Los Angeles, California.

1972 The last wild Arabian oryx was shot dead.

1978 The first zoo-bred oryx were returned to Jordan.

1982 A protected oryx herd was established in Oman.

1996 Poachers start illegal hunting of wild oryx.

1998 The re-introduced oryx in the region numbered 500.

2000 Herds are re-established in Oman, Saudi Arabia, Jordan and Israel.

Many zoos run educational programmes, aimed at keeping the public aware of the world's rapidly dwindling stock of wild creatures. It is important that people living in the big cities of Europe or North America can see an African elephant or an orangutan first hand, in order to keep some kind of bond with the animal kingdom.

Find out!
Choose one type of animal and research its natural environment. Compare this with how it lives in a zoo. What are the differences? What efforts have been made to recreate its habitat?

The Arabian oryx, once on the verge of extinction, was saved by an operation that bred the animals in captivity and then released them back into the wild.

Chapter 3

RELATIVE VALUES

A crucial question in any debate about cruelty centres around how much pain animals actually experience.

Pain is registered by special nerves called receptors. The 'higher' forms of life, such as apes or dogs, have a central nervous system based upon a spinal cord and a brain. This is a complex system which enables them to remember a certain amount and, up to a point, 'think'. 'Lower' forms of life such as sea anemones have a much simpler chain or network of nerves, and no proper brain. They are conscious in a much more basic way and operate purely as a result of instinct or physical reaction.

Creatures at different levels clearly experience pain in very different ways. Scientists can test the electrical and chemical functions of any nervous system, but they cannot do more than imagine what that creature experiences and feels.

So, is cruelty to all animals equally wrong, or is it relative to the complexity of the life form? Is killing a mouse in a trap as cruel as killing a fox in a trap? Is it equally cruel to swat a wasp, or to put out pellets which kill garden slugs?

How does cruelty to animals rank when compared with cruelty to people? Should we be really concerned with ill-treatment of animals in a world where children are mistreated? The one concern does not rule out the other, but we all have to decide where our priorities lie.

What do we make of a campaigner for animal rights who is at the same time a racist? In 1999, when a whale hunt was organised by a Native American people called the Makah of Washington State, USA, local papers received torrents of racist abuse, saying that it was the 'Indians' who should be harpooned.

Adolf Hitler (1889–1945) had six million human beings murdered during the Second World War, but he was a keen dog-lover and vegetarian.

Question
Pets are now being called 'animal companions' by some people. Is this giving them the dignity they deserve, or is it sentimental nonsense?

Find out!
Find out the names of six animal welfare organisations. What are their current campaigns? Do you agree with them?

ENVIRONMENT AND WILDLIFE

The influence of human beings on the planet is obvious. Humans have tamed and hunted animals, removed their habitats and even caused some animals and plant species to disappear altogether. We mourn the loss of animals such as the dodo, and conservationists fight to save the giant panda.

Humans are not to blame for all the changes that happen to the world's wildlife, though. There are climatic and geological events that we have no control over. Volcanoes erupting, meteorites crashing to Earth and solar activity can all affect the planet in a way that makes our influence seem insignificant.

There is also an argument that even extinctions are part of the natural process of evolution, even if they are brought about by human activity. If an animal cannot adapt to changing conditions then surely it is appropriate that the species should die out, making way for more 'successful' species or variations? This is, after all, part of the process by which humans came to evolve.

• Today, nearly 6,000 animal species around the world are recognised as endangered or threatened.

Question
It may be a shame if an animal becomes extinct, but does it really make the world a poorer place? If so, why?

Helpers clearing up the coastline after a spill from an oil tanker. Such leaks have a devastating effect on sea birds and other forms of marine life.

NOWHERE TO RUN

The spread of humans over the planet has led to the clearance of forests, the draining of wetlands, the building of cities, roads, airports and pipelines. This has improved human life in many ways. How many of us would really like to return to the dirty, disease-ridden streets of the Middle Ages? Birds such as kites thrived in those times, scavenging the town rubbish dumps. Today, kites may be very rare in Britain, but at least we can now lead healthy, comfortable lives. Indeed, our convenient lifestyle allows us the time and resources to protect animals and think about conservation.

Tropical rainforests such as this have been cut down, destroying many animals' natural habitats in the process.

However, it cannot be denied that their habitat is being destroyed. Human development may affect their ability to breed or find food. It may block the routes along which they migrate. It may create problems of overcrowding, as more and more animals are concentrated in the only small pockets of territory where they are able to survive. They become cut off from other groups, which inhibits breeding.

- It has been estimated that half the world's wetlands have been destroyed, mostly in the last 100 years, through agricultural drainage.

- Tropical rainforests are among the richest of all animal habitats. It is quite possible that within 50 years, no significant areas of rainforest will remain.

Not all habitat change has been disastrous, though. Many wild animals, such as foxes, have learned to live in cities. Cities and towns often support more birds than the surrounding countryside.

> **What would the world be, once bereft Of wet and of wildness? Let them be left!**
> Gerard Manley Hopkins (1844–89), English poet

FOULING THE NEST

In the last 100 years, humans have polluted the planet on which they live. Factory waste and sewage have flowed untreated into rivers and seas. Fertilisers have drained off farmland into rivers. In 1989 the tanker *Exxon Valdez* covered over 2,400 km of Alaskan coastline with crude oil – one of the worst-ever spillages, but just one of many. The air has become filled with exhaust fumes from traffic and smoke from factory chimneys, creating choking smog. Chemicals have combined with water vapour in the air to create acid rain. Nuclear accidents have leaked invisible clouds of radioactivity over the countryside. Ocean floors have become dumping grounds.

Pollution is bad enough for humans, but for animals it often spells death. Oil spillages leave seabirds and seals coated in foul-smelling, sticky black oil. Fish can no longer survive in about 4,000 Swedish lakes as a result of acid rain. Rivers become open drains empty of wildlife: no fish, no otters, no plants. Marine creatures become sickly and deformed.

The issue of pollution is now being tackled in many places. Fish are now swimming in European rivers such as the Thames, which was once notoriously filthy. Laws control factory waste and exhaust fumes. But the big clean up is just too expensive for many countries. And anyway, it may be too late....

ARCTIC MELTDOWN

The climate is changing. It has changed before, of course. Climate change may have hastened the end of the dinosaurs, and many creatures never survived the last great Ice Age. This time, however, it is changing very quickly, and evidence suggests one reason for this is human pollution of the planet's atmosphere. Global warming is already creating problems for wildlife. Polar bears are starving in the Arctic, as warmer oceans change the breeding patterns of the creatures they hunt for food. Is this just part of a natural, long-term pattern, or one more example of unnecessary interference with the environment?

Some people believe that the significance of global warming is being exaggerated. Life on Earth has adapted to climate change before, they say, and will again.

Question
Would you be prepared to stop using a car to reduce air pollution, particularly the emission of 'greenhouse gases' which add to global warming?

PEST CONTROL

Farmers have always tried to kill the animals they regard as pests attacking their crops. Some 4,000 years ago the Chinese tried using ants to kill insect pests on orange-tree leaves. This was an early example of biological pest control.

In 1939 a Swiss scientist discovered a powerful chemical insecticide, dichlorodiphenyltrichloroethane (DDT). It was devastating when sprayed on crops. It killed the insects – and often the birds that ate them and the animals that ate the birds. DDT ended up in humans, too. Animals, including humans, are all interdependent, part of complex food chains and webs. If one link in the chain is broken, the others are affected.

DDT was widely banned as a result, but many other pesticides are still used on crops today. The world needs efficient crop production, say the sprayers. Efficiency doesn't come into it, say the critics. They claim that only 0.01 per cent of the pesticide actually kills the pest. The rest poisons the environment.

One hundred years ago crop yields were low, weeds grew through wheat fields and insects caused widespread damage. Today the situation has been turned around. Could that have happened without chemical spraying? Is the solution to find more efficient and less harmful chemicals rather than oppose them altogether?

Question
Given the choice of a treated apple with a clear skin or an untreated one with a marked skin, which would you buy and why?

" As crude a weapon as the cave man's club, the chemical barrage has been hurled against the fabric of life. "

Rachel Carson (1907–64), US naturalist and writer

IN STRANGE LANDS

Biological pest controls, in which one animal is introduced to destroy another, tend to be more friendly to the environment than chemical controls. One common method is to introduce new predators from one region of the world to another. While many of these introductions have been successful, they have frequently had unforeseen or extreme effects and have often brought about the extinction of native animals.

DEADLY TRADES

A major threat to wildlife comes from collectors and traders. Birds' eggs or butterflies are collected as rare objects. People are paid to steal nests or eggs, or to trade in live parrots or birds of prey. Approximately 50,000 apes and monkeys and millions of birds and fish are shipped around the world each year, with large numbers dying in transit. There is a major trade in ivory from elephant tusks, in animal skins and in rhinoceros horn or other parts of wild animals widely used in traditional Asian medicines. Tourists buy jewellery made from endangered corals or turtle shells.

International trade in endangered animals and products is now illegal, controlled by the Convention on International Trade in Endangered Species (CITES). Despite this, poaching and smuggling remains widespread.

- The people who kill elephants for their tusks are often desperately poor. Can they be blamed for poaching? Is it the fault of some national governments, turning a blind eye to lawbreaking? Governments may lack the resources to control the situation, or may have lost the ability to enforce the law during war or famine. Is the trader to blame, or the consumer at the end of the line?

Question
Is it best to ban the trade in ivory completely, or to control and limit it? Should the tusks of culled elephants be sold legally?

CONSERVATION AND CARE

One way to reverse the decline in wildlife numbers is to impose and enforce a ban on fishing or hunting. A world moratorium on whaling has allowed numbers of some species to return from the brink of extinction.

Stocks of fish have declined rapidly in many parts of the world. Fishery bans have now been imposed on the formerly rich fishing grounds off Newfoundland in Canada, and strict quotas (catch limits) have been set in Europe. Most fishermen know that stocks are declining, but complain that the laws imposed are unfairly enforced or unworkable. Zoning off oceans into sections makes little sense when shoals of fish are on the move, and limiting catches by species, when all catches include fish of many species, makes the fisherman's job very difficult.

The pressure on wildlife stocks from hunting and fishing may be reduced by the creation of fish farms, fur farms or crocodile hide farms. Fish farms have proved to be a useful source of food, but they can also foster fish diseases and parasites, and waste from fish farms has been known to poison nearby rivers, killing much of the wild stock. Fur and hide farms are sometimes criticised as cruel and unnecessary; fur farming was banned in Britain in 1999.

WILDLIFE HAVENS

Another weapon in the conservation war is the protection of even small wildlife breeding sites and colonies. At a local level, their protection is often difficult to enforce. It has been argued that in the future the farmer's role as a guardian of the countryside could be as important as that of food producer.

National parks and wildlife reserves play a crucial part in providing a refuge for wild animals and have saved countless endangered species; the Galapagos Islands, for example, are a protected natural habitat that tourists may enter and enjoy, but only with an official guide. Many national parks have good schemes for monitoring and

Wildlife parks have played an important role in saving endangered species and providing a refuge for wild animals.

protecting wildlife, and in this way they help to educate foreign tourists at the same time as helping the local economy.

Question

Organisations such as the Royal Society for the Protection of Birds (RSPB) say that the current farming environment is hostile to wildlife. Farmers claim that they are the true guardians of the environment. Who do you think is right?

Find out!

Find out where your nearest wildlife reserve is and what schemes they have for preserving local animal species.

HUNTING, FISHING AND WHALING

In some parts of the world, people still live by hunting wild animals, by eating insect grubs or gathering honey and food plants from the forest. They may bring down their prey with bows and arrows, spears, blowpipes, nets or harpoons. Traditional hunter-gatherer communities are now few and far between, but in regions such as Central Africa, many people are forced by war or famine to take 'bush-meat'. Fishing is another story. Many millions of people around the world still depend upon fish as an everyday source of food.

The difference between hunting for survival and killing animals for profit is reflected in international agreements which ban whaling by modern fleets, but still allow the native peoples of the North Pacific and Arctic to harpoon a few whales each year for their own use.

Question
Which is more important, the traditions of hunter-gatherer peoples or the preservation of wild animals?

Some whale species are endangered and whaling is largely banned. Some whales may be killed for 'scientific research'. Even so, some of this whale meat still seems to end up on the commercial market.

HUNTING FOR PLEASURE?

Many people hunt and fish just for pleasure, calling such activities 'field sports'. In many countries, hunting activities are officially controlled, limited or banned – but laws are not always strictly enforced. There are great differences between the laws of one country and the next, although international treaties do outlaw forms of hunting which endanger the survival of threatened animal species.

People may hunt on foot or on horseback, using hounds to track down the animal and kill it. Stag hunting, fox hunting and hare coursing are all examples of hunting with dogs; badgers too are dug out from their setts. The animals hunted vary from one continent to another, with species of deer, antelope, wild sheep and goat among the most common. In most countries, the chief method of hunting is by shotgun. Shooting is also the normal way of killing wildfowl or game birds, such as pheasants. Here, the dogs' role is to retrieve the shot birds.

> **"Properly conducted hunting (with dogs, birds of prey, ferrets), shooting, and fishing can make a positive contribution to the ecological balance. The pleasure involved is not in suffering but in the sport – in which the element of suffering is deliberately minimized."**
>
> Countryside Movement: Charter on the Welfare of Animals, UK Countryside Alliance

Fox hunting is one of the most controversial sports in Britain. Is it a centuries-old tradition that should be upheld, or a cruel and unnecessary pastime that should be outlawed?

What kind of pleasure do people get from hunting? Supporters of fox hunting often say that they enjoy the open air and the horse riding – but they could always support a 'drag hunt', in which a trail of scent is laid out for the hounds to follow instead of a live fox. Is it really the pursuit and taking of life which hunters enjoy? After all, first-time hunters in Britain are often smeared with the blood of the dead fox, rather like some primitive ritual.

Hunters often dress in special clothes. Some of these may serve a practical purpose, such as camouflage jackets, boots or warm hats. But some hunters still wear fancy costumes, such as the red ('hunting pink') jacket of England, or the green jacket and feathered hat of southern Germany. Why do people dress up like this? Perhaps to emphasise that they are part of an old tradition, or out of a desire to show off their status.

PRO AND ANTI

Hunting is often justified by the claim that it rids the countryside of vermin. Vermin is the name given to animals that are regarded as pests – foxes, for example, because they kill poultry. If so, say critics of hunting with dogs, why not simply shoot the animals? Would that not be more humane?

> **Question**
> Is it more morally acceptable to only hunt animals that can be eaten?

> **Question**
> Does enjoyment of hunting depend on the animal having a chance of escape?

> **Question**
> Is hunting a basic human instinct, or learned behaviour?

> **❝ What kind of pleasure can it possibly give to a man of culture … when a splendid beast is transfixed by a hunting spear? ❞**
>
> Marcus Tullius Cicero (106–43 BC),
> Roman statesman

The hunting of some animals can indeed help to conserve wildlife, by keeping numbers down to a sustainable level. If animals overbreed, there may not be enough food available to ensure their survival.

Using hunting to reduce the total number of wild animals is called culling. Culling is not only used to conserve species, but also to serve human interests in managing natural resources, for example when seals are killed to protect fishing stocks.

Question

Is culling animals to protect the fishing industry less defensible than culling animals to protect their own future?

AT THE SHOOT

In what might be seen as a reverse of the culling principle, many game birds are actually bred in order to be shot and eaten. They live in managed environments protected by gamekeepers. Without shooting, these birds would not exist, nor would the countryside in which they live. Reared grouse or pheasants probably lead a better life than chickens on a poultry farm. They are well fed and protected from predators. But they are not raised just for food. They are raised to be shot for pleasure, by people who pay large sums of money to do so.

FUR AND SKIN

Many animals are shot or trapped for their fur or skin. Big cat species, from leopards to ocelots and lynx, are all used to make coats, hats or rugs. Trapping, which aims to preserve the fur with as little damage as possible, may be cruel if an animal becomes tangled in a snare or is left injured or starving for days on end. Crocodiles and snakes are killed too, and their skin is used to make bags, wallets, belts and shoes. This is hunting for commerce rather than pleasure. Its devastating effect on wild species has led to the growth of fur farms (see page 28) and the development of 'fake furs', made from synthetic fibres.

Question

In the 1980s and 90s many fashion designers and consumers boycotted fur in fashion; now fur is being shown again on the catwalks. What does this tell us about people's reasons for wearing or not wearing fur?

> ❝ Giving up fur was not an entirely deep or meaningful statement. ❞
>
> *The Guardian*, February 2000

THRESHOLDS OF PAIN

Hunting with dogs, and other forms of extreme pursuit, increase the amount of stress and panic experienced by animals. Arguments about how much pain animals experience (see page 22) are crucial to the debate about hunting and fishing. If fox hunting is banned, then should fishing not be banned too? Yes, say campaigners. Hooking a fish and depriving it of the water it needs to breathe is cruel, even if the fish is thrown back alive. No, say anglers. Fish are simpler life forms which do not experience the levels of pain and distress known to the 'higher' animals.

Question
Many people are more shocked by the killing of a gorilla than by the killing of a fish. Why do you think this is?

One of the major debates about activities such as angling centres on how much pain the fish actually feel. Unfortunately, this is something we can only guess at.

Chapter 5

THE JAWS SYNDROME

We kill dangerous animals such as sharks, crocodiles or snakes in order to protect the public. But often there are other motives, too.

- Bravery: sometimes people like to prove their courage by coming face to face with dangerous animals.
- Revenge: if an animal has harmed or killed a person, others want to take revenge, not simply on that one animal, but on any of the species.
- Fascination: we like to demonise dangerous animals, as happened in the 1970s films *Jaws*, about a great white shark; humans seem to be fascinated by the power and strength of such animals.

All these attitudes lend animals human characteristics which they do not possess. It is a kind of sentimentality in reverse. A shark does not think, 'Yum, yum, a human being!'. It simply registers movement, water disturbance, blood in the sea – and follows its instincts. To blame a shark or lion for attacking a human is meaningless.

> " [Ahab] piled upon the whale's white hump the sum of all the general rage and hate felt by his whole race from Adam down.... "
>
> *Moby Dick*, by Herman Melville (1819–91)

> " When a man wants to murder a tiger, it's called sport; when the tiger wants to murder him it's called ferocity. "
>
> George Bernard Shaw (1856–1950),
> Irish writer

> " When we speak of unnecessary suffering, we must answer the question, 'Unnecessary to what?' If some suffering is necessary to an activity that we have independent reason to think legitimate, such as eating meat or controlling vermin, then it should be permitted. "
>
> Countryside Movement: Charter on the Welfare of Animals, UK Countryside Alliance

34 **ANIMAL MATTERS**

ON THE FARM

Welcome to the countryside, the rolling farmland, the peaceful fields and streams. Cattle and sheep graze peacefully – just as nature intended. Or perhaps not.... Most countryside is no more 'natural' than a city garden or park. Farmers have felled trees, ploughed up grassland and drained marshes. And of course the sheep and cattle you can see are not wild species, but creatures produced by selective breeding (see page 10), solely for the benefit of humans. They are human inventions, and few of them could survive long in the natural world.

This is a humane rearing system for veal calves, in which they have straw bedding and freedom to move. Often veal calves are raised in small crates and kept in darkness.

CHANGING TIMES

One hundred years ago, cattle were still given personal names; today they are given an ear tag with a number. Farming was on a smaller scale. Whether it was more humane is open to debate. Some traditional farming methods – such as over-feeding geese with maize to enlarge their livers – are now condemned as barbaric by campaigners, even if they are accepted by many consumers.

The chief change in farming methods today is one of scale. Ever since the 1920s, many countries have been applying the production methods used in factories to farming. Farming has become an industry. This period has seen crop pests being killed off by chemicals and cows being milked by machines rather than by hand. Many farms keep chickens caged in long production lines ('batteries'), rather than leaving them to forage freely in the farmyard.

BATTERY CHICKENS

Battery chicken farming is still the most common method of raising poultry and producing eggs. It keeps prices low and so the products are purchased in huge quantities at supermarkets.

Since the 1920s, the farming industry has undergone some radical changes, including pest control with chemicals.

Battery farming keeps costs down, but the conditions in which the birds are forced to live and lay eggs have caused an outcry, and many farmers now keep free-range chickens.

Battery farming is opposed by many people, however. Thousands of birds are crammed into small cages and are made to lay many more eggs than they would naturally. One method which encourages laying is to use artificial lighting sequences, so that the bird is confused by bright lights or left in gloomy darkness. The confined birds develop diseases which are treated by antibiotics. Traces of these remain in the meat and the eggs.

Battery production is now banned in some countries, including Switzerland and Sweden. In others it is being phased out.

VEAL PRODUCTION

The methods used to produce veal are not intended to increase the quantity of meat, but to give it a certain quality. Calves are separated from their mothers and raised in crates which allow very little movement. These conditions are required to make veal, a pale and tender meat – and the development of strong muscles through movement would only make the flesh tougher. The calves are kept in darkness for most of the day and are fed with a low-nutrition milk substitute which keeps their flesh white.

MAD COW DISEASE

One consequence of factory farming brought about a sharp decline in Britain's beef industry in the 1990s. Companies began to produce prepared feeds for calves based upon meat and bone-meal from sheep and cattle, even though cows are herbivores (grass-eaters). The unexpected result was a deadly, as yet untreatable cattle disease called bovine spongiform encephalopathy (BSE or 'mad cow disease'). This affected the brain and central nervous system of cattle. Before long, there was strong evidence that a fatal disease could be passed on to humans who ate infected meat. The suspected link was named new variant Creutzfeld-Jakob disease (nvCJD). The BSE problem was eventually tackled, but few countries would buy British beef, and scientists do not know how many nvCJD cases might yet appear.

DRUGS IN THE SYSTEM

Antibiotic drugs may have helped control animal diseases and saved many animals' lives, but they have been greatly overused in the farming industry. Once antibiotics are in the food chain, they pose a risk to human consumers. Our bodies become used to the drugs, reducing the effectiveness of antibiotics prescribed for human diseases.

Hormones, the chemicals produced by animal and human bodies to control basic functions, are also used to regulate artificially the lives of farm animals. A hormone called bovine somatropin (BST) is produced naturally by cows, but supplementary injections may increase milk yields by up to 10 per cent. This is common practice in the USA, where it has been declared safe, but it is still resisted by the countries of the European Union. The USA has taken international action to force the EU to accept imports of BST-treated dairy products.

Question
What are the implications of allowing one country to force another to accept imports of meat or dairy products against the wishes of its government, by using international trading agreements?

Question
Is it acceptable to use hormones to boost milk production, when there is no shortage of milk?

USER-FRIENDLY FARMING

Many farmers have reacted to scares about factory farming. They have turned away from the widespread use of chemicals and from the production-line treatment of animals. Organic (untreated) crops and fodder are now produced on many farms. Chickens are often kept 'free-range', able to move more freely. Cattle are not treated with hormones. Antibiotic use has been greatly reduced. There is a ready market for free-range eggs and similar produce.

However, such goods are more expensive to produce. Non-organic farmers say that they can only meet the cheaper prices demanded by the public if they continue to use chemicals. Either people must be prepared to meet the higher costs, or else governments must give financial support to farmers in order to make it worth their while to use friendlier farming methods.

It would seem that the worst excesses of factory farming belong in the past, as governments have already introduced stricter controls over conditions and practices. The trouble is, such laws are often brought in as a reaction to mistakes that have already happened – and abuses are still widespread. All the time, science is bringing about new possibilities which companies pressurise farmers to adopt. This is nothing new, but the pace and scale of change makes it hard for us to keep up with the implications.

Question
Do new scientific developments, such as genetic engineering, mean that diseases such as BSE are more or less likely to occur?

Find out!
What arguments are put forward by supporters of organic food and how are these countered by those who oppose it?

Find out!
What campaigns are currently being conducted to clean up factory farming? How successful have they been so far? Do you agree with them?

LIVING WITH LIVESTOCK

The debate about farming methods leads on to even bigger questions. Should we be raising farm animals at all? When it comes to the efficient use of land, a crop of soya beans yields 22 times more protein per hectare than a herd of cattle – and at a much smaller cost. These are crucial figures for a crowded, hungry world.

Natural habitats such as rainforests and woodlands have been deforested to develop grasslands for grazing livestock. This can lead to the formation of deserts and changes in climate in the long term.

Thirty-nine million turkeys are slaughtered each year in Britain, most for the traditional Christmas dinner.

Grazing animals worldwide account for approximately three per cent of greenhouse gases in the atmosphere.

On the other hand, cattle dung can be used to produce electricity and to fertilise the soil. Milk from cows and goats provides an essential source of protein and calcium, especially in the developing world.

Question
Is the production of meat necessary or a waste of resources?

Find out!
What is the price difference in your local supermarket between:
- **Free-range, barn and battery eggs?**
- **Meats from organic and non-organic farms?**

MEAT OR MURDER?

The life of most farm animals is very short. Most creatures are slaughtered for meat when they are young or when they are no longer of any use. In most countries the slaughter of animals is now closely regulated – for reasons of public health and also to ensure that the death is humane.

In a typical year, Britain slaughters about:
- 2.3 million cattle
- 14.2 million pigs
- 18 million sheep
- 39 million turkeys
- 13 million ducks

TO THE SLAUGHTER

Even to convinced meat-eaters, the first sight of an abattoir, or slaughterhouse, may be a distressing experience. Animals are often goaded and pushed to their death in a clear state of distress. However, we cannot really know what they experience.

Animals are normally secured and then stunned before they are killed, for the blood must flow out of the body before it is dead if the carcass is to be fit for the butcher's shop. Stunning may be caused with a blow to the skull or by passing an electric current through the brain. Most scientists claim that animals become unconscious as soon as they are electrocuted, but some critics believe that they may first experience pain. The veins and arteries are then cut open so that the blood flows out.

Jewish and Islamic religious beliefs require animals to be slaughtered according to particular rituals. No stunning is permitted. The arteries and veins are severed rapidly with a sharp knife. If the meat is of the right type and slaughtered in the correct way, it may be declared religiously lawful and fit to eat – *kosher* to Jews, *halal* to Muslims.

> " ... The time will come when men such as I will look upon the murder of animals as they now look upon the murder of men. "
>
> Leonardo da Vinci (1452–1519), Italian artist and engineer

Is meat murder?

'Meat is murder' is a common slogan of animal rights campaigners. Slaughter is certainly bloody and violent. But 'murder' means the killing of another human being, so it cannot be applied to animals without twisting its literal meaning. What the slogan suggests is that animal slaughter is *equivalent* to human murder, a crime of equal weight.

This brings us back to the basic ethical dilemma – where do we draw the line? Do all living things have equal status? Is it murder to eat microscopic animal life living in the oceans and, if so, is it also wrong to eat carrots?

This is taking the argument to an extreme and it may be concluded that we shouldn't take any life, even plant life. This leaves us with the problem of what to eat! Alternatively, we could conclude that taking the life of any animal is not wrong and we should just eat what we like, regardless of how it gets to our plates.

Certainly there are valid arguments for eating meat. Most people enjoy meat and it is a good source of protein and iron. From puberty onwards women need a diet that contains iron or to take iron supplements. A sensible compromise may be to eat less meat and only when it has been produced in a manner we, as individuals, find acceptable.

> 66 **My grandparents were farmers, they lived on the land. They ate loads of bread and dripping, pork crackling, roast beef – you name it. They both lived to a ripe old age.** 99
>
> Lizzie, English Midlands

Question
Should people only eat meat if they are prepared to kill the animal themselves?

Find out!
Some people say that meat provides nutrients that are important for human health. Investigate what these are in different meats and what vegetarian and vegan foods can provide alternatives. Are there any that cannot be replaced by such diets?

ARE VEGGIE BURGERS BEST?

Why do people become vegetarians? Some are put off by the very idea of eating animals. Others are following religious teachings. The majority of vegetarians choose their diet because they believe it is healthier. There is a proven medical link between the eating of animal fats and diseases of the heart and arteries.

Some people compromise by only eating white meat or fish. Champions of a carnivorous diet say that humans have been eating meat since they first existed, that this is our natural state. As part of a balanced diet it is perfectly healthy. There is plenty of evidence to suggest that oily fish are among the healthiest foods humans can eat.

Vegans extend their vegetarian diet to exclude eggs and dairy products. Provided there is a balanced diet with alternative sources of protein, this is perfectly healthy. Many will not wear leather or other animal hides, preferring plastic or other synthetic-fibre footwear and jackets. Few vegans are able to screen themselves from all animal products, for these may be used in the manufacture of a wide range of everyday items, from the glue used by bookbinders to the films we seen in the cinema.

> " Tell me what you eat, and I will tell you what you are. "
>
> Anthelme Brillat-Savarin (1755–1826), French politician and gourmet

> " Ninety-seven per cent of consumers continue to eat and enjoy meat. The meat market is worth £12 billion and is the biggest single food market in Britain. "
>
> British Meat

> " Living consistently and compassionately as a vegan is an affirmation of life.... "
>
> Vegan Outreach, USA

Question
Should diet be a matter of individual choice, or should it be regulated by laws?

ONE MAN'S MEAT ...

... is another man's poison, according to the old proverb. The French may eat frogs legs and snails, the Koreans may eat dog. The Chinese may eat owl, monkey or snake, the Greeks often like octopus. Australian Aboriginals may eat insect larvae called witchetty grubs, and some African peoples feast on the big grasshoppers called locusts. This might not be what we are used to, but is it any more strange than eating jellied eels or a hamburger? Many Chinese find the idea of eating cheese distasteful – it is, after all, a kind of sour, solidified old milk.

Many of our attitudes towards meat are cultural, based on history or religion (see page 12–13). Sometimes we no longer even know why we eat one meat and not another. Many French and Belgians like to eat horseflesh, while their neighbours to the north and east normally do not. One theory offers an explanation for this.

About 2,000 years ago the ancient Germanic peoples (ancestors of Germans, Dutch, Scandinavians and English) used to sacrifice horses to their gods and then eat the flesh. Along came Christian missionaries, who forbade this practice as pagan. However, for the peoples living in France and Belgium, horses had no religious significance, pagan or otherwise, so the practice of eating them was not banned there and it therefore continued.

Amazonian Indians making a caterpillar stew. Every culture and people has a different diet and different views on what it is acceptable to eat.

IN THE LABORATORY

Many millions of animals are bred not in the farmyard or in the wild, but in the science laboratory. These include rats, mice, guinea pigs, cats, dogs, rabbits, monkeys, apes, birds, fish and frogs. The animals are rarely kept in the labs for their own benefit. They are there to be experimented upon by humans. The term 'guinea pig' has been adopted to describe the living subject of any scientific experiment, animal or human.

For hundreds of years, students of biology have learned about animal physiology by dissecting, or cutting up, animals. This starts in many school classrooms and continues through university. Critics say that other teaching methods, including examination of living creatures and of realistic models, would serve the purpose just as well for most pupils.

Vivisection means 'cutting alive'. It originally only described experiments which involved dissecting or cutting into living creatures. Today the term is used more widely, to cover a range of experiments using live animals which take place in laboratories – the injection of chemicals, drugs or viruses, freezing and burning, electrical shocks, mutilation, surgery.

Vivisection normally takes place to test products for potential hazards to humans, or for biological and medical research. It is one of the animal issues that generates very strong feelings, both for and against.

> **" Animal research is vital to medicine. "**
>
> Jack H. Botting and Adrian R. Morrison, article in *Scientific American*, 1 February 1997

> **" I found vivisection horrible, barbarous and above all unnecessary. "**
>
> Carl Jung (1875–1961), Swiss psychiatrist

PRODUCT TESTING

Many animals are used to test products used by humans. The products may vary from shampoos and cosmetics to medicines, detergents, foodstuffs and additives. Will they cause irritation to the skin or eyes? Might they cause diseases such as cancer? Do they have any unpleasant side effects? What happens if they are used to excess?

Shampoo may be dripped into the eyes of rabbits and, for many years, dogs were forced to inhale tobacco smoke, to see if they developed cancerous lungs. Animals are even used to test the effect of weapons – bullets, explosives, gases and poisons.

- The companies paying for such research argue that it is necessary to safeguard the consumer. They point out that in industrialised countries, most governments have passed laws regulating conditions and the humane treatment of laboratory animals.
- True, say the critics, but the laws are very limited and do not cover many species commonly used in experiments. Besides, they say, animal testing is largely unnecessary in the days when computer models and specially cultured human cells can be used in laboratories.

- Perhaps the critics' most important claim is that testing simply doesn't work – it is a waste of time. It is certainly true that many products which have eventually proved to have disastrous side effects upon some humans were first tested on animals, but showed no similar adverse effects. In many cases, humans and other animal species are quite simply too dissimilar. The connection between lung cancer and cigarettes was validated not by making beagles smoke all day, but by studying human population trends and habits.

Some cosmetics manufacturers have responded to public opinion and some goods are now labelled 'not tested on animals'.

Question
Does the end product have to validate the research? Is it worse to use animals for testing cosmetics than, say, medicines?

> **After a great deal of research, we discovered that we could develop new, innovative and safe products without testing them on animals.**
>
> Kenneth Landis, president of the Benetton company

MEDICAL RESEARCH

Medical researchers have long used animals in a search for remedies and treatments which will work for humans. As early as 1667, Jean-Baptiste Denys attempted – unsuccessfully – to give a teenage boy a transfusion of lamb's blood.

A more modern example might be the use of mice to create antibodies. An antibody is a chemical naturally produced by the body to fight off disease. Scientists can join the cell from a tumour with a cell that can produce antibodies and let it develop in a mouse. The mouse's body now produces antibodies, used to fight a certain type of cancer. The mouse has, in effect, become a factory for antibodies, in order to benefit humans.

Today this practice is no longer really necessary, as the antibodies can be created by other methods. It has therefore been banned in Britain and some other countries, but is still being used in the USA.

Critics argue that biomedical research using animals is an example of humans regarding themselves as a 'master species'. They have a word for it – 'species-ism', similar to 'racism'. They claim we have no right to exploit our fellow creatures in this way. Nonsense, say supporters. Biomedical research using animals has advanced the cause of science immeasurably and has already saved countless human lives. If you could save your life by killing a mouse in a mousetrap, would you?

> **❝ Without laboratory experiments, my son would be dead by now. Don't talk to me about the rights of mice.... ❞**
>
> Rosa, New York City, USA

Question

If you were opposed to animal experiments, but your life depended on a new product produced in animals, what would you say to your doctor?

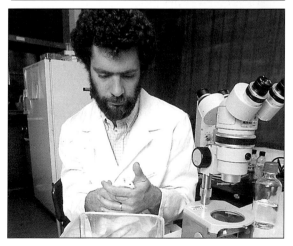

Laboratory experiments on animals can result in medical advances. Does this make it acceptable?

A GENETIC REVOLUTION

The antibodies-from-mice process has been made possible by advances in genetic engineering. Since the 1970s, genetic engineering has transformed biomedical research.

All living creatures are naturally programmed, rather in the same way as a computer. The programme is found within living cells, in strands called chromosomes. These are made of a chemical called deoxyribonucleic acid (DNA). The minutest details of the programme are carried in hundreds of thousands of genes.

Scientists can now add extra genes into DNA. An animal can be made to carry genes from another species of animal, or even a plant. It is then said to be 'transgenic'. One of the main aims of such research is to provide humans with life-saving drugs.

Question
Is using a transgenic animal to provide us with life-saving drugs any different from using a cow to provide us with milk?

Dolly the sheep – the first mammal successfully cloned from an adult cell – with her lambs. This experiment raised many issues about the possibility of cloning human beings.

CROSSING SPECIES

Genetic engineering and other developments in biomedical research have brought animal and human physiology into a much closer relationship. For example, it is now possible for an animal organ, such a pig's heart, to be transplanted into a human body.

Such operations remain very difficult, and raise many practical problems. For example, by increasing close contact between different species, we increase the chances of diseases leaping the species barrier, just as the human disease nvCJD seems to have done from its origins in cattle-borne BSE (see page 38).

Even more complex than the medical problems are the ethical dilemmas raised by this area of research. Is it right that animals should be used to provide spare parts for humans? Where do the borders between animals and humans really lie? Might we be in the process of destroying the essence of what is human?

DOLLY THE SHEEP

Cloning is the creation of a new living organism from the cells of one other, just as cuttings are routinely taken from plants. The new organism has an identical genetic make-up to the original. In 1997 it was announced in Scotland that a lamb (named 'Dolly') had been created by cloning. A cell had been removed from the udder of a sheep. It had been joined to an unfertilised egg whose DNA coding had been removed. The fused cells were then grown in the lab and finally implanted into a female sheep, which gave birth – to an identical copy in every way of the original sheep.

It now seems that scientists are gaining control of the life process itself. Where will it end? Well, why would anyone *want* to clone *humans*, asked one scientist when questioned. The lesson of history is, that if it can be done, it will.

> **Question**
> Are scientists 'playing God' by the processes of genetic engineering?

> **Question**
> Is having a pig's heart in a human body so very different from eating a pork chop?

ANIMALS OF THE FUTURE

Scientists are not altering animal DNA just to save human lives. They are also attempting to create new animals for the benefit of farmers. Just as scientists want to create bigger, juicier or hardier vegetables, they want to produce woollier sheep, meatier cattle…. The farmers of the future may well rely on genetic engineering and cloning to create the herds of the future.

- What is the problem with that? Surely, it is little different from the selective breeding that has taken place since farming was invented. Isn't selective breeding a form of genetic engineering?

- Well it is, but one that is subject to natural controls. Modern genetic engineering is intrusive and less natural. Do we want to follow that road? It could have unforeseen results. Evolution has always been achieved slowly by natural selection. Legal controls and responsible science will prevent mistakes, say some, but we should remember that powerful commercial companies are behind some experimentation and they have different priorities to independent scientific bodies.

> ❝ **How can we trust scientists? They said nuclear power was safe, they said eating beef was safe…. Why must they keep interfering with nature?** ❞
>
> Caro, environmental campaigner, Scotland

> ❝ **All this talk of Frankenstein farming is so much nonsense. We are just continuing what farmers have always done, selecting the best characteristics of the animals and plants we breed.** ❞
>
> Tim, geneticist, England

ANIMAL RIGHTS?

In the late 1700s, political campaigners began to talk about human 'rights'. They meant that every human being deserved certain basic conditions in order to live – social equality, for example, and freedom rather than slavery. Most governments of the day ridiculed such ideas, but in the 200 years that followed, the notion of rights became generally accepted. People claimed the right to education, to a healthy life, to democracy, to freedom from poverty. Today, many people claim that animals, too, have rights. What do they mean?

Anti-vivisectionist protesters on a demonstration march in central London.

> **The day may come when the rest of the animal creation may acquire those rights which never could have been withholden from them but by the hand of tyranny.**
>
> Jeremy Bentham (1748–1832), English philosopher

TOWARDS LIBERATION

Animals are part of the same living network as ourselves. Surely they have just as much right as we do to life and protection? Indeed, it might be argued that the case for animal rights is made even stronger because they are unable to make their own case. We must act for them.

Some might point out at this stage in the argument that animals are not really dumb. It has been shown that more intelligent animals, such as dolphins, have relatively complex patterns of communication. Chimpanzees have been taught the gestures of human sign language.

Animal rights might be said to include humane treatment, the right to life, the right to a habitat in which wild creatures can survive. Other people would go much further, though. They do not choose simply to highlight questions such as the humane treatment of farm animals. They want humans to stop exploiting animals in any way whatsoever, and to treat other species with respect. This radical viewpoint is referred to as 'animal liberation'.

> **❝ ... as we recognise human rights, so too should we recognise the rights of the great apes? Yes. ❞**
>
> Jane Goodall (b. 1934), English ethologist

Human rights are backed by laws, agreements, treaties. Many animal liberationists wish to see animals accorded similar legal rights to those of humans. This is no pipe dream – there is already a growing body of animal law.

The question of animal intelligence is a serious one when weighing up animal rights issues. We know that some animals, such as dolphins, have relatively high levels of intelligence. Does this entitle them to more rights and better treatment?

NO MORALS, NO RIGHTS

THE PECKING ORDER

Animals cannot have rights, counter others. The whole notion is just one more example of well-intentioned people claiming that animals are like humans, when they quite clearly are not. Human rights depend upon reciprocal action – on 'you doing something for me' and 'me doing something for you'. Human rights, some argue, cannot exist unless they are accompanied by *duties* towards society. Each individual must be responsible for his or her actions.

An animal, however, acts from instinct and cannot be responsible for its actions. It may be very intelligent: it may learn how to press a computer keyboard to gain food, or even use simple tools. It may have similar DNA. But it cannot understand the bigger picture, for only humans have a sense of morality. Without that understanding, there can be no *rights*, legal or otherwise. There can only be legal *status*.

The natural world has a hierarchy, an order in which animals can be graded according to complexity of life form and intelligence. If animals have rights, are all animals equal? Do animals with bigger brains have more rights than ones with no real brains at all? Is an orang-utan, which can look so like a human, the equal of a sea snake?

Animal rights necessarily conflict. Surely the rights of the lion conflict with the rights of the zebra it needs to eat? Does a parasite such as a tapeworm have as much right to survive as the host animal?

If animal rights are to be formally recognised by humans, then long-held ideas of the law must be restructured to accommodate them.

> **Great fleas have little fleas upon their backs to bite 'em,**
>
> **And little fleas have lesser fleas and so ad infinitum.**
>
> Augustus de Morgan (1806–71), English mathematician and logician

> **All animals are equal, but some animals are more equal than others.**
>
> George Orwell (1903–05), English novelist

CONFLICTS OF INTEREST

Animal rights clearly conflict with human rights, too. Do the rats and fleas which carry the deadly bubonic plague have a right to survive? Should a motorist who accidentally runs over a hedgehog or a toad face the same penalties as someone who runs over a human being?

Question
Should we concentrate on resolving issues on human rights before we worry about the rights of animals?

Such animal-human conflicts may seem to be extreme examples, but others are already matters of public debate. The Masai people have herded cattle on the Kenya-Tanzania border for hundreds of years. However, large areas of their pastures are now occupied by wildlife reserves and national parks. Access to traditional grazing lands is now lost or restricted. Are the rights of the Masai to a livelihood of a lesser order than those of elephants and giraffes? Conflicts of interest such as these need a practical political solution which can be backed by law.

On a wider, industrial level, many African countries suffer from extreme poverty and need the revenue from cattle ranching. This would mean encroaching on the habitats of wild animals. Should they reduce their economic potential in order to preserve the environment?

A Masai herds cattle over the land of lions and zebra. Which should have precedence? Can they live together?

ANIMALS AND ACTIVISTS

All kinds of people take action on animal matters. There are campaigners against cruelty to animals and vivisection. There are supporters of animal welfare. There are people who work for conservation and the protection of endangered species. There are supporters of animal rights and animal liberation. There are people who hunt, shoot and fish for pleasure or for food. There are people who work with animals in the belief that they will make scientific discoveries that will benefit humanity.

Many people have direct contact with animals on a day-to-day basis. There are millions of pet-owners. There are the farmers, who must decide how their animals are raised and whose own livelihoods depend on them. There are the people who transport animals, the people who sell animals, the people who slaughter animals.

Animal rights campaigners in London, demonstrating against the export of live animals. Peaceful demonstrations such as this are one of the ways in which people show support for their beliefs on animal issues.

METHODS OF ACTION

All these people may take action in support of their beliefs and interests, either as individuals or as part of campaigning or practical organisations or trade unions. There are thousands of organisations around the world whose chief concerns are animal matters, many of them directly opposed to each other.

Activists may restrict their action to personal example. They may show kindness to animals or choose an organic meat-based, vegetarian or vegan diet. They may take more practical action, by raising funds for animal causes, volunteering to work with injured animals or carrying out conservation work.

Most campaigners and lobbyists (people who put their arguments across to companies or politicians) follow peaceful and lawful means. They may organise a boycott, for example, refusing to buy the products of a company which tests its products on animals. Other campaigners are prepared to take more direct action provided it is non-violent. They may picket an abattoir or a laboratory, or lie down in front of lorries transporting calves. Such action may, however, be illegal.

Question

Is it justifiable to break human laws in defence of animals?

Find out!

There is an increasing body of animal law in Britain. Find out what these laws are and how they are enforced.

Recent changes have granted some primates legal rights similar to those of humans. Is this granting them a status to which they have no claim?

How Far Is Far Enough?

Other direct activists may make a conscious decision to break the law or risk violence. They may throw a brick through the window of a lorry, or burn down a place where animals are bred for experiments. A hunter on horseback may launch a physical attack upon a hunt saboteur. Such actions may be described as terrorist, in that they are using violence to promote a climate of fear in order to further their beliefs or pastimes. In the USA, the Federal Bureau of Investigation (FBI) has identified animal liberation supporters as posing one of the most potent terrorist threats to the state.

Action may not only risk human life, but also those of other animals. When animal liberation supporters recently released large numbers of mink from a British fur-farm, they made the news and achieved publicity for their cause. However, they also ensured the death of many wild animals that these mink would hunt. They also risked upsetting the fragile and already threatened balance of the river ecosystems of southern England.

> ❝ **These animal liberation people are irresponsible, they have got things completely out of proportion.** ❞
>
> Ceri, battery hen farmer, Wales

> ❝ **I'm glad the government is shutting down fur-farms, but I'm really angry they're paying compensation to these murderers.** ❞
>
> Lisa, animal liberation campaigner

Demonstrations are not always peaceful; the strength of feeling aroused by animal matters sometimes gives way to violence.

Question
Is it justifiable to risk a human life in the name of animal liberation?

CHANGING PERSPECTIVES

The questions on animal issues raised in this book have arisen for a number of reasons. There has been an increased awareness of environmental problems. The revolution in genetics has made us increasingly concerned about animals and science. Are animals to be simply carriers of spare parts with which to repair human bodies? Farming catastrophes such as 'mad cow disease' have raised worries about farming methods.

Current economic and political concerns have led us back to the fundamental questions which were being addressed by religious teachers and philosophers thousands of years ago. What are humans and what are animals? Are they one and the same?

FACING THE FUTURE

The aim of all life forms, including humans, is to continue the existence of their own kind. As a species, though, we are unique in having the wisdom to examine and predict the effects of our behaviour. This brings with it a special responsibility. In the developed world we have the privilege of choice, which comes from economic wealth. The decisions we make regarding our relationships with other creatures on this planet should be based on knowledge and an understanding of a broad range of issues.

Whether we believe animals have rights or not, we know that the world would be a very different place without whales crashing through the waves or wolves howling in the forests.

> " The realisation that our small planet is only one of many worlds gives mankind the perspective it needs to realise sooner that our own world belongs to all its creatures. "
>
> Arthur C. Clarke (b. 1917), English science-fiction writer

Find out!

Carry out a survey of people in your school or college. Which animal organisations do they support? How do they rate animal matters in comparison with other current issues? How many don't eat meat? How many support hunting and fishing?

ORGANISATIONS AND HELPLINES

Animal Action
PO Box 170
Middlesborough, TS1 4YN
Tel: 07801 365944

Animal Aid
The Old Chapel
Bradford Street
Tonbridge
Kent, TN9 1AW
Tel: 04732 364546

Commission in World Farming Trust
Charles House
5a Charles Street
Petersfield
Hampshire, GU32 3EH
Tel: 01730 68070

Friends of the Earth (UK)
56-58 Alma Street
Luton
Bedfordshire, LU1 2PH
Tel: 020 7490 1555

Greenpeace (UK)
Canonbury Villas
London, N1 2PN
Tel: 020 7865 8100

International Animal Rescue
Animal Tracks
Ash Mill
South Molton
Devon, EX36 4QW
Tel: 01769 550277

Royal Society for the Prevention of Cruelty to Animals (RSPCA)
Supporter Care Department
Causeway
Horsham
West Sussex, RH12 1ZA
Hotline: 0870 55 55 999

People for the Ethical Treatment of Animals (PETA)
PETA Europe Ltd
10 Parkgate House
Broomhill Road
London, SW18 4JQ
Tel: 020 8870 3966

WWF (UK)
Panda House
Weyside Park
Goldalming
Surrey, GU7 1XR
Tel: 01483 426444

IN AUSTRALIA

Greenpeace (Australia)
Level 4 34-39 Liverpool Street
Sydney
NSW 2000
Tel: 2 9261 4666

IN NEW ZEALAND

SPCA Auckland Inc
50 Westney Road
Mangere
Auckland
Tel: 9 256 7300

Animal Welfare Services
PO Box 93109
Waitakere City
Auckland
Tel: 9 839 0400

WEBSITES

Animal Aid:
www.animalaid.org.uk

Bills before UK Parliament: www.parliament.
the-stationery-office.co.uk/pa/pabills

Conservation International:
www.conservation.org

Countryside Alliance:
www.countryside-alliance.org

Countryside Commission:
www.countryside.gov.uk

Countryside Commission for Wales:
www.ccw.org.uk

Farmers' Union of Wales:
www.fuw.org.uk

Friends of the Earth:
www.foe.co.uk

Government information UK:
www.open.gov.uk

Greenpeace:
www.greenpeace.org

National Anti-Vivisection Society:
www.navs.org

National Farmers Union:
www.nfu.org.uk

People for the Ethical Treatment of Animals:
www.peta-online.org/uk

Royal Society for the Protection of Birds:
www.rspb.org.uk

Royal Society for the Prevention of Cruelty to Animals:
www.rspca.org

Scottish Animal Liberation Front:
www.atlantica.co.uk/ecology/animal lib

Scottish Parliament:
www.Scottish.Parliament.co.uk

UK Parliament:
www.parliament.the-stationery-office.co.uk

UK statistics:
www.statistics.gov.uk

UN Earthwatch:
www.unep.ch/earthw.html

Vegan Society:
www.vegansociety.com

Vegetarian Society UK:
www.vegsoc.org

Welsh Assembly:
www.wales.org.uk

World Conservation Union:
www.iucn.org

Worldwide Fund for Nature:
www.panda.org

Zoological Society of London:
www.zsl.org

abattoirs 41, 56
abuse and ill-treatment 20, 22
acid rain 25
activists 55-57
animal liberation 52, 55, 57
animal rights 51, 52, 53, 54
animal skins 27, 43
animal testing 46
animal welfare 7, 17-18, 55
apes 8, 20, 22, 27, 45

battery farming 36, 37, 40
birds 17, 24, 27, 45
BSE ('mad cow disease')
  38, 39, 49, 58
Buddhism 13
bullfighting 16

campaigning and
  campaigners 18, 22, 33,
  36, 42, 51, 55
captivity 15, 19, 20
cattle 10, 35, 36, 39, 40
chemicals 25, 36, 39, 45,
  47
Christianity 12, 13
circuses 20
climate 25, 40
cloning 49, 50

cock-fighting 15
conservation 7, 23, 24, 27,
  28, 32, 56
Creutzfeld-Jakob Disease
  (nvCJD) 38, 49
cruelty 15, 17, 22, 55
culling 32

Darwin, Charles 9
Denys, Jean-Baptiste 47
DNA 48, 50, 53
disease 37, 38, 39, 43, 46,
  49
dissection 45
'docking' 18
Dolly the Sheep 48, 49
drugs 45, 48

endangered species 21,
  23, 27, 28, 55
environment 9, 23, 25, 26,
  54, 58
ethics 13, 20, 42, 49
evolution 9, 23, 50
experiments 7, 45, 57
extinctions 23, 26, 27

farms and farming 11, 14,
  15, 17, 18, 19, 25, 26, 28,
  35, 36, 38, 39, 40, 45, 50,

52, 55, 58
factory farming 7, 38, 39
'field sports' 30
fish farms 28
fishing 7, 28, 29, 30, 33, 55
food chains 26, 38
fox hunting 30, 31, 33
fur farms 28, 32, 57

Galapagos Islands 28,
gamekeeping 17, 32
Gandhi, Mahatma 11
genetic engineering 10, 39,
  48, 49, 50
Global warming 25
greenhouse gases 40

habitats 21, 23, 24, 28, 40,
  52, 54
hare coursing 30
Hinduism 13
Hitler, Adolf 22
horse riding 31
human rights 52, 53, 54
hunters and hunting 7, 10,
  12, 14, 18, 23, 28, 29, 30,
  32, 33, 55, 57

insecticides 26
insects 9, 24, 25, 26

instinct 34, 53
ivory 27

Jainism 11, 13
Judaism 12, 13, 41

laboratories 7, 15, 45, 46, 56
laws and legal rights 17, 30, 43, 50, 52, 53, 54, 56, 57
leather 43
livestock 17, 40

meat 7, 19, 42, 43, 56
medical research 45, 47-48, 49
menageries 20
Middle Ages, the 20, 24
morality and moral guidelines 8, 14, 53
Muslims 13

national parks 28, 54
neglect 19
nuclear accidents 25

Operation Oryx 21
organic 39, 40, 56
overbreeding 32

pesticides 26
pets 14, 17
  exotic 20
poaching 27
pollution 25

predators 26, 32
product testing 46

rainforests 24, 40, 58
religion and religious guidelines 11, 12, 13, 14, 41, 43, 44, 58
rituals 16, 31
RSPCA 17, 18, 20
RSPB 28
science and scientists 13, 22, 39, 41, 47, 50, 58
selective breeding 10, 35, 50
shooting 30, 55
slaughter 41, 42
slavery (human), 17
smuggling 27
stag hunting 30

taboos 13
Thames, River 25
tobacco 46
totems 12, 13
traditions 31
transmigration 13,
transportation and transit 19, 27, 55, 56
trapping 32

veal 37
vegans 43, 56
vegetarians 11, 22, 43, 56
veterinary care 19, 20
vivisection 45, 55
volunteer work 56

whaling 27, 29
wildlife 7, 23, 25, 27, 32
  reserves 28, 54
Worldwide Fund for Nature 8

zoos 20, 21